M000274498

# APPALACHIAN Christmas ABCs

Written by
## Francie Hall

Illustrated by
## Kent Oehm

The Overmountain Press
JOHNSON CITY, TENNESSEE

ISBN-13  978-157072-328-5
ISBN-10  1-57072-328-1
Printed in the United States of America
1 2 3 4 5 6 7 8 9 0

Dedicated to
Ellie, Wade, Simone, and Hayden
*Francie*

Dedicated to
Juliet

*Kent*

A is for the *Appalachian Mountains*.
These hills and lofty peaks stretch
along the eastern part of the USA.
Christmas celebrations in these Appalachian
Mountains this book will portray.

B is for *Bonfires*.
Ablaze on hilltops during blustery nights,
these towering infernos warmed all who came
to join hands and sing
around the glowing flame.

C is for *Church Choirs.*
Softly they sang, "Silent night, holy night.
All is calm, all is bright,"
As candles flickering in the windows
cast a shimmering light.

D is for *Decorations.*
Popcorn, berries, paper chains, and a foil star
were strung and hung with loving care.
Everybody gathered around the tree
and worked hard to do their share.

E is for *Excitement*.
Participants shouted, "Christmas Gift!"
expecting a treat to be tossed their way.
Like a game of tag, "Christmas Gift!" was
played excitedly throughout the winter day.

F is for Feasting.
Families feasted on roast turkey, smoked ham,
and fluffy biscuits that were just grand.
There were chestnuts and sweet potatoes that
had been stored in boxes full of sand.
Favorite desserts were boiled custard,
pumpkin pie, and apple-stack cake.
Everyone chattered and ate
until their tummies would ache.

G is for *Gifts.*
Stuffed in homemade woolen stockings were
gifts so simple, plain, and rare—
An orange, a stick of candy, a carved wooden
sling-shot, or a rag doll with frizzy hair.

H is for *Hunting*.
Through the cold of a snowy morn,
the men of the family tracked their prey
of rabbits, turkeys, and other game
to eat on Christmas Day.

I is for the *Irish* of Scottish descent.
Since bringing their holiday traditions
to our shore,
Appalachians have enjoyed these customs
and have added many more.

J is for *Jigs*.
While dancing all night long,
Merry-makers lifted their spirited voices
in joyful song.
They pushed the furniture against the wall
and took down the feather bed.
Fiddlers fiddled and friends did dance
until their faces turned bright red.

K is for *Kinds of games played.*
Favorite ones were
"Cross Question, Silly Answer" and
"Please or Displease."
In "Bite the Candy," the winner with a kiss
his partner did appease.

L is for a *Legend* told on Christmas Eve.
When the Christ Child came to Earth
for all to see,
Even donkeys and cows gathered around the
manger on bended knee.

M is for *Mistletoe.*
Shot from an oak tree, this festive ball of green
was hung from the ceiling.
Underneath the mistletoe, a boy kissed a girl,
expressing the love he was feeling.

N is for the "*New Christmas,*" December 25th.
Many years ago on the calendar
this new date was set.
Today this date for celebrating Christmas
is still kept.

O is for the "*Old Christmas,*" January 6th.
Some folks celebrated the twelve days
between the "New" and the "Old."
They visited, sang, and walked to church
through the cold.

JANUARY 6

P is for *Pageants*.
Children dressed up in paper costumes
and recited verses telling the story
About angels, shepherds, three kings,
and God's glory.

Q is for *Quilting bees.*
Women busily stitched bits of fabric
into colorful patches
While they shared holiday news about
births and weddings in snatches.

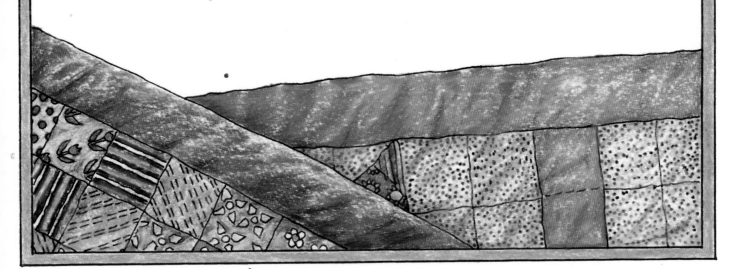

R is for *Relatives.*
Families traveled over rutted roads
for distances great and small.
While jostling in ox-drawn carts,
each clung tightly so as not to fall.

S is for *Serenadin'*.
Young'uns snuck up on neighbors
by lantern light.
They fired shotguns and rang cowbells
and caused quite a fright,
Demanding treats on a late winter night.

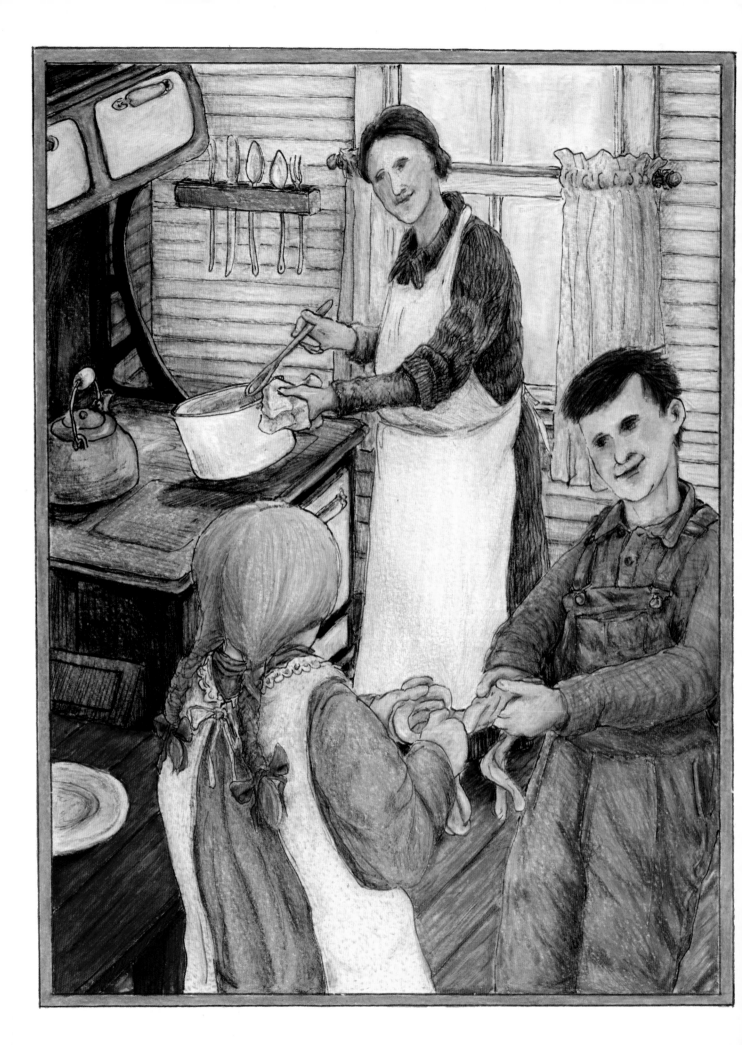

T is for *Taffy pulls.*
Boiling molasses was poured
into plates to cool.
Boys and girls with greasy hands
pulled it tighter than thread on a spool.
Tangled up in a golden ropey swirl,
The boys hoped to put their arms
around their favorite girl.

U is for *Unity*.
If wintertime brought hardship
and less food in the larder.
And staying warm and fed
became even harder,
Neighbors pulled together,
sharing what they could,
Working side by side
for the greater good.

V is for "*Visit From St. Nicholas.*"
This very old poem describes the gift-giver
St. Nick and his reindeer and sleigh
Delivering bundles and bundles of toys
to children on Christmas Day.

W is for *Whittling*.
Craftsmen carved the Christ Child
with a block of holly and a knife of steel.
This smooth and satiny figure was a symbol
of the Christmas spirit people did feel.

X is for *"X" marks.*
Children would mark an "X" on the calendar,
counting off each day.
Advent meant twenty-four days to go,
and Christmas was on its way.

Y is for the *Yule log*
Or "backstick" as it was called.
A hickory stump was soaked in water
and placed in the hearth to burn.
Families clustered around the fire
and shared their favorite stories in turn.

Z is for the *Zephyr breezes*.
Soft winds gently blew
Christmas wishes so sweet.
"Peace on Earth, Good Will to Men,"
on every street.

MERRY CHRISTMAS